My House Is Different

Kathe DiGiovanni

Hazelden

Special thanks to
Nancy Johnson
Program Coordinator
Rockford Memorial Hospital

First published January, 1986.

ISBN: 0-89486-342-8

Printed in the United States of America.

Editor's Note:
   Hazelden Educational Materials offers a variety of information on chemical dependency and related areas. Our publications do not necessarily represent Hazelden or its programs, nor do they officially speak for any Twelve Step organization.

Once upon a time there was a small boy named Joe. Joe lived with his mom and dad in a house on Rainbow Road. The outside of Joe's house was like everyone else's on Rainbow Road, but inside, things were different.

It was especially different when Joe's dad came home from work. Joe's dad always said he needed a couple of drinks to relax after work. Joe thought that was okay because his friend Jimmy's dad sometimes had a drink after work, too.

But Joe's dad acted different after a few drinks. He yelled at Joe and his mom and broke things around the house. Joe worried when his dad left the house and stayed out late. Joe saw his mom cry and get angry. At times she became so angry she yelled at Joe.

Joe felt scared when his dad drank. He was afraid his dad might hurt his mom. Other times Joe worried his dad might not come home at all. Joe got mad when his dad drank because other fathers didn't act like that. Some dads played ball with their kids and took them places. But Joe's dad didn't, and Joe felt disappointed a lot. Sometimes Joe thought it was his own fault.

Joe thought if he were a better boy, maybe Dad wouldn't drink so much and Mom wouldn't yell. Joe often felt lonely and confused. But he was ashamed to talk to his friend Jimmy about it. Maybe Jimmy wouldn't like him anymore. Most of the time Joe didn't talk to anybody except his dog, Fuzzy. Joe needed Fuzzy.

At times, Joe felt sorry for his dad and wanted to help him, but didn't know how. One day Joe's mom said she was going to visit someone and wanted Joe to go with her. They went to visit an alcoholism counselor, someone who knows a lot about people who drink too much. The counselor asked Joe if he was ready to do something so he could feel better. Joe said yes. He was ready to do something for himself.

On the ride home Joe thought about what his new life would be like. When he arrived home he said, "Come on Fuzzy, let's take a walk on the road to our new life and find out what it will be like."

Joe and Fuzzy walked down Rainbow Road until they met a farmer. The farmer said he planted corn seed in the field, but nothing had grown. He said he felt helpless because he could do nothing to make the corn grow. Joe felt helpless when he could not stop his dad from drinking. Joe thought, "We are often helpless about things."

Joe and Fuzzy continued down the road. The sun on Joe's face was bright and hot. Joe thought, "It would be nice if it would rain. Rain would cool things off a bit and help the corn grow. But only God can make it rain."

Joe felt good knowing God took care of things like that. Suddenly, even though the sun was still shining, a few drops of rain began to fall. Joe was feeling happy; happy for himself and for the farmer whose corn seed needed rain to grow.

After the rain stopped, Joe and Fuzzy walked on and saw a cracked egg on the roadside. Inside the egg was a tiny bird with its eyes barely open. Joe felt sorry for it and wanted to help.

He thought the mother bird should love and take care of her baby. He could remember feeling sad when he thought his mom and dad didn't love him. Joe picked up the bird. It felt so light and soft and easy to break. The bird reminded Joe of himself. It trembled with fear and helplessness the same way he did sometimes. Joe sat under a tree with the bird in his lap.

Joe closed his eyes for just a minute, and suddenly he heard chirping. He opened his eyes to see the baby bird flapping its wings, trying to fly. Its mother looked on proudly, knowing her baby would soon fly. Joe felt better because the mother did love the baby bird after all.

Joe and Fuzzy walked on. Soon they came upon a clear pond filled with ducks. The ducks were fighting over some bread at the edge of the pond, each one only thinking of itself. Joe thought of the times he had not considered others and thought only of himself.

Joe looked into the water at his reflection and decided he would try to be a more caring and kind person. He knew this would not be easy, but he was ready to try. Joe asked, "Will you please help me, God?"

As Joe walked away from the pond, he was thinking about his house on Rainbow Road, and his family. He thought about how angry he used to be at his parents and all the times he had taken out his anger on Fuzzy when Fuzzy had done nothing wrong.

Joe and Fuzzy followed the road into a thick forest. They were surrounded by the smell of the pines which were all around them. Joe heard a loud growl that sounded like a bear. Frightened, he and Fuzzy hid behind a tree.

Suddenly a strong, deep voice said, "Come out please, I won't hurt you." Joe and Fuzzy peeked around the tree and saw a large brown bear holding his toe. "I'm sorry if I scared you," the bear said. "I just stubbed my toe and it hurts."

Joe and Fuzzy were a little nervous, but walked over and sat by the bear.

"Don't be afraid," said the bear. "I used to go around and purposely scare all the animals. One day, during a big wind storm, I got scared. The sky was a very dark purple, and the wind blew so hard I thought the trees might fall on me. I called out to God, 'If you will save me I will help all the animals of the forest.' "

"Then the storm began to fade away, the trees stopped moving, and the sky became brighter. Since that time, I've become friends with all the animals. I would like to be friends with you, too."

Joe and Fuzzy liked the bear right away. As Joe thought about the story, he wanted to tell his mom and dad how sorry he was about the way he used to act. He decided to make a list of the people he wanted to say he was sorry to, and he felt better.

Joe looked ahead and saw a big brown wooden bridge over a river. As he and Fuzzy walked over the bridge they saw their reflections in the glassy water.

Joe looked down at his reflection and thought he saw a change in himself. "I will look at myself every day," he said. "And when I've done something wrong, I will admit it." Joe thought this was a great idea and was beginning to understand more about himself and the road to a better life.

The road broke up into many paths ahead, and Joe and Fuzzy had to decide which one would lead them home. In a tree overhead Joe saw an owl with bright golden eyes, and asked, "Which way should I go?"

"Hoot, it's true I'm a wise old owl, but I can't solve your problem. When I need some answers, I ask God for help."

Joe thanked the owl and bent his head to pray. "God, can you please show me the way?"

Joe had faith that God wouldn't lead him in the wrong way. So he and Fuzzy started walking. It wasn't long before Joe recognized the path and knew he was going the right way.

After walking down a long path, Joe could see his house in the distance on Rainbow Road. He thought about all the things he had learned about himself, and decided he was a good person. "I don't have to be sad all the time!" Joe shouted aloud. "Let's go, Fuzzy, we can run the rest of the way."

Just then they saw a wishing well beside the path. Joe threw a penny in and made a wish. "My wish is to understand myself more each day, and I wish we can all be a happy family again."

Joe looked up and saw his house ahead. It looked so much brighter and friendlier. He and Fuzzy ran straight for the door. Joe felt good to be home even though he didn't know what to expect when he got inside.

As Joe walked into the house, he didn't know if his dad would be drinking or if his mom would be upset. But Joe knew he himself was different. He was responsible for his own feelings and attitudes and he knew only he, with God's help, could change them. For Joe, this was a new beginning!